OFFICIALLY NOTED

W9-ANI-860

REFLECTIONS ON THE WALL
The Vietnam Veterans Memorial

With Forewords by

Jan C. Scruggs,

John P. Wheeler III,

Gen. William C. Westmoreland, U.S. Army (Ret.),

and James Quay

REFLECTIONS ON THE WALL
The Vietnam Veterans Memorial

Photographs by the Smithsonian Institution's
Office of Printing and Photographic Services

Introduction and Narration by
Edward Clinton Ezell

Design by James H. Wallace, Jr.

WITHDRAWN
FROM THE RODMAN PUBLIC LIBRARY
RODMAN PUBLIC LIBRARY

STACKPOLE BOOKS

975.3
R 33 2
B - 2

Copyright © 1987 by the Smithsonian Institution

Published by
STACKPOLE BOOKS
Cameron and Kelker Streets
P.O. Box 1831
Harrisburg, PA 17105

All rights reserved, including the right to reproduce this
book or portions thereof in any form or by any means,
electronic or mechanical, including photocopying,
recording, or by any information storage and retrieval
system, without permission in writing from the publisher.
All inquiries should be addressed to Stackpole Books,
Cameron and Kelker Streets, P.O. Box 1831, Harrisburg,
Pennsylvania 17105.

Printed in the United States of America

10 9 8 7 6 5 4 3 2 1

Library of Congress Cataloging-in-Publication Data

Reflections on the wall.

   1. Vietnam Veterans Memorial (Washington, D.C.)—Pictorial
works. 2. Washington (D.C.)—Buildings, structures, etc.—
Pictorial works. I. Ezell, Edward Clinton. II. Smithsonian
Institution. Office of Printing and Photographic Services.
F203.4.V54R44   1987   975.3   86-23151
ISBN 0-8117-1846-8

RONALD J JOHNSON · A
ANGEL R LUNA · CHARLES H
JA Jr · HARRY T POLAND · RO
NSON Jr · STEPHEN J SZIJJAR
R · DARRELL W WILSON · TH
MARK L ENGLISH · LEON V
Y · ALBERT J McAULIFFE · JOE
· RAYMOND C CLARK · DAV
N · RAYMOND N HERRINGT
WELL · EDMOND SAN MARC
MON · JAMES F HARRIS · JAN
VICH · DALTON B LOWERY ·
MILLER · TIMOTHY J McCART
ELL · CHARLES H BALL · JACK
WITT · RAY B DeBUSK Jr · G

CONTENTS

An aerial view of the Vietnam Veterans Memorial
in Washington, D.C., showing the arms of the
250-foot-long black granite wall.

FOREWORD BY
Jan C. Scruggs

The Healing Stone. A Shrine of Reconciliation. The Wall. America's Vietnam Veterans Memorial has been given many names.

During a visit to the Memorial you may see a grown man weeping. Or a young woman leaving flowers. Or a child placing a poem near one of the names. These individual moments make the Memorial special.

America has other great and inspiring national memorials. But the Vietnam Veterans Memorial, with nearly 60,000 names engraved on its black granite wall, is unlike any other. No other memorial so occupies a place in the heart and soul of the nation as does this simple, reflective wall.

The idea that led to the creation of the Vietnam Veterans Memorial began to develop in my mind while I was studying psychology in graduate school. America needed a memorial to the men and women lost in Vietnam in a war that many Americans preferred to forget. Such a memorial could help veterans and the entire nation recover from the Vietnam experience.

But in 1977 this was just the dream of one Vietnam vet—a college student with no money or political connections. In 1979, after I saw the movie The Deer Hunter, the dream became an obsession.

No one remembered the names of the people killed in the war. I wanted a memorial engraved with all the names. The nation would see the names and would remember the men and women who went to Vietnam, and who died there.

The creation, development, and construction of the Vietnam Veterans Memorial ultimately involved two U.S. presidents, the U.S. Congress, hundreds of volunteers, a dedicated full-time staff, and hundreds of thousands of Americans who donated the nearly $9 million needed to build it.

At times, it seemed as though Divine Providence intervened. I remember agonizing how we could ever carve so many names on the planned memorial. Then, unexpectedly, a young inventor came to our office. Larry Century claimed to have perfected a technique using photo stencils, which, with some developmental work, could do the job.

As often happens in Washington, politics nearly destroyed the Memorial. Powerful members of Congress rallied to stop the construction of what one Vietnam vet called a "black gash of shame." During an emotional meeting in 1982, the project was saved when Retired Army General Michael Davison suggested the addition of a statue to the Memorial site.

During the many difficult times that faced this historic enterprise, some great Americans helped make the Memorial a reality. These individuals include former Attorney General Elliot Richardson, former Secretary of State Cyrus Vance, journalists Hugh Sidey and James Kilpatrick, as well as numerous members of Congress, especially U.S. Senators Charles McC. Mathias, Jr. and John W. Warner, and Congressman David E. Bonior.

The success of the effort is truly remarkable.

Our primary objective—to provide a lasting acknowledgment of service and a welcome home to America's Vietnam Veterans—has been achieved. After the divisiveness of the Vietnam War years, the Vietnam Veterans Memorial now stands forever proudly on Washington's Mall as a symbol of our nation's resilience and unity.

For nearly four years, the photographers at the Smithsonian Institution documented the impact of the Vietnam Veterans Memorial. Their photographs illustrate the emotions that the Vietnam War continues to generate.

Author Herman Wouk once wrote: "The beginning of the end of war lies in remembrance." The Vietnam Veterans Memorial serves as a remembrance for all Americans, especially for the veterans of Vietnam. Like the Memorial itself, this is a book to be remembered.

Jan C. Scruggs is President of the Vietnam Veterans Memorial Fund. He is the author of To Heal a Nation: The Vietnam Veterans Memorial *(Harper & Row, 1985).*

ROBILOTTO · TODD A HANDY · DANA H ROESNER · RICHARD ROMERO · RONALD L SALVA
SCULLEN · ERWIN B SIMS · WILLARD SKAGGS Jr · RONALD A SLANE · MARK E SMITH ·
MPSON · RONALD J STILLEY · CLIFFORD G STOCKTON · DANNY M STONEKING · DANNY G
TALL · JOHN M THOMPSON · ARISTIDES SOSA · CARREL J TITSWORTH · MICHAEL R TRAVIS ·
VELVET Jr · LARRY H WALDEN · GARY W WATKINS · TERRY LEE WEAVER · PAUL E WEST ·
WETHINGTON Jr · DARRELL E WHEELER · LARRY A WIDENER · JOSEPH J WILLIAMS · LEONARD J
W WINGET · DANNY S YOUNG · WILLARD F YOUNG · VIRGIL L WILLIAMS · HOMER L AKE Jr ·
E ALSMAN · HOWARD H ASHFORD · RICHARD L BORGMAN · FRANK L BROWN · KENNETH ·
CARLI · MELVIN CARRILLO · RONALD J D CASPER · DAN E CHARLES · JAMES M DARBY ·
M L COLON-PEREZ · PHILIP M CREWS · MICHAEL L CHARLES · VINCENT A DATENA · FRANK R D
DISMUKE · RONALD D DUCKER · EDWIN R EDWARDS · MICHAEL J FARRIS · ERNEST E FAWKS ·
A FOSSETT · FRANCISCO FRANCO · JACKIE W GARNER · LAWRENCE L GASKA · RICHARD S G
GOURDINE · HAROLD HOLMES · LAWRENCE E JONES · WILLIAM A JORDAN · VICTOR A JUSTIN
H NESTLERODE · GARY A LARSEN · DONALD W LATTMAN · JIMMY F LEHMAN · PETER MITCHEL
L MOORE · DIMITRIOUS C McCALL · DONALD A NAHODIL Jr · DAVID W KNOUSE · HENRY NO
OGLE · RODRIGO VELAZQUEZ-FELICIANO Jr · DOMINGO ORTIZ · JIMMIE E PARKER · DANIEL L
N W PERRY · EDDIE LEE PLEASANT · M RAYMOND REEVES · HAROLD E REKAU · SAMUEL D RIDE
G ROSS · THOMAS P RUSSO · THOMAS F SMITH Jr · RICHARD C SPENCER · ALFRED W SPEYER
T SWYMER · DENNIS H THOMPSON · JOHN W VAN SANT · KENNETH L OLDHAM · EARNEST S V
VELSHAN · JAMES E WILLIAMS · RAY H WOODS · RANDALL L YOUNG · ROBERT W ABERNATHY
E W ACHOR · THOMAS B ADAMS · TERRY E ALLEN · CURTIS E BAKER · GEORGE L BARBER III ·
ELL · LEONARD O CHANDLER · PRENTIS B BOYKIN Jr · DAVID K BRUNING · ALAN D CARSON ·
DO F BILDUCIA · RICHARD L CLAVERIE · JAMES CROCKRAN · DOUGLAS D CROWE · JAMES R DA
S G DE FOSSE · ADRIAN L DEL CAMP · CHARLES C DUNN · BERNARD J FLEMING · WILLIE F FOSTE
A GALLAUGHER · EZRA GAVIN · EDWARD HENRY · DAVID P GOLDSMITH · GARY D HALL ·
HARLESS · MICHAEL D GEISE · RAMON SANCHEZ HERNANDEZ · ROBERT J HODAL · GARY O HO
D G HUDSON · WILLIE H HUNTER · GEORGE R HUTCHINSON · ISRAEL L INGRAM · ROBERT E JAC
ST JOHNSON · RICHARD JOHNSON · RONALD B JONSSON · DONNY R KIDD · ROBERT W KOIVU
D M LENTZ · VERNON LEE LEUNING · D G LEWIS · JAMES C SWANN · WILLIAM P MASON ·
K ROSS · DENNIS H MUTZ · PATRICK F O FRANK A OSTER · GARY C PARKINSON ·
N F PENDERGRASS · ROBERT E POE · TE RANDALL · ANTHONY E REED · RONALD J RHODES
O PENA RIOS · JEREMIAS ROMAN · ED MILAN · CAMILO J SANCHEZ · DONALD B SAUNI
HY R SCHROEDER · EDWARD A SCHUL W STEVENS Jr · LORENCE M LUNDBY · VOYD E TI

OWEN F NEUMYER • JACK W
GEORGE A SANDERS • JERRY K
PHILLIP T WILEY • JOHN S
VITO V BRUNO • GERALD O
JOHN W FARNESTY •
MICHAEL C KIRBY
Washington DC

FOREWORD BY

John P. Wheeler III

The photographs in this volume include beautiful images of the Vietnam Veterans Memorial. Much of their beauty comes from the reflective quality of the Memorial's black granite wall.

During the creation of the Memorial, a series of unexpected and graceful turns of events occurred. These events combined to make the Memorial a powerful symbol and instrument of healing.

Before construction of the Vietnam Veterans Memorial, those of us working on the project knew the wall would be shiny and reflective. But no one anticipated the sharp, true, and expansive mirror quality of the wall. The high polish of the black granite surface reflects blue sky, green trees, the Washington Monument, the Capitol Dome, the Lincoln Memorial, and the expressive faces of visitors who approach the Wall.

The power of a mirror image lies in the fact that it shows us as others see us. Confronting such an image often leads us to peer inside ourselves: "Oh, that image isn't the real me . . . ," or, "I look so sad . . . and that is how I feel." Reflections thus reveal us to each other and to ourselves.

With great power, the images in this book reveal Americans to themselves, in faces that express pride of service, woundedness, grief, hope, and commitment to live up to the best that was in the lives of the Americans who gave their lives in Vietnam.

John P. Wheeler III is Chair of the Vietnam Veterans Memorial Fund.

LARRY J NICHOLSON
JOHN D RHODES III
VICTOR B SUTTON
RICHARD P VALADEZ
JOHN C ARCHBOLD
JOHN M BLACKFORD
PHILLIP D BURFOOT
SAMUEL C COPELAND
LARRY C DAVISON
HENRY C ETTEL Jr
CURTIS L HENDRICKSON
JOHN A KALIVAS
CLIFFORD J T LEFLER
LARRY W MARTIN
BRUCE A PANKUCH
JAMES M NESSELROTTE · DANIEL G O'CONNELL
JOHN H PRIEST Jr · ISRAEL RODRIGUEZ
RONALD E SIMPSON
LUIS J SIMANCAS · JAMES I WOODS
JOHN DE MEY
CRAIG H HANSEN
GLENN R JENNINGS · JIM E JENNINGS
ROBERT C MAHAN
JAMES E PARKER
TIMOTHY A SHOBER
HAROLD J FINNEY Jr
CHARLES G GRAY
EDWIN PEREZ
RICHARD L DAVIS
MARVIN M BURNS

FOREWORD BY

William C. Westmoreland, General, U.S. Army (Ret.)

I am proud and honored to pay tribute to the gallant Vietnam Veterans who served their country, especially those who gave their lives maintaining freedom.

Few have experienced the anguish that I have felt for those men and women who did in Vietnam what the leadership of the country asked them to do—and did it well—and who in return were ignored and often abused by their fellow countrymen.

Most Vietnam Veterans have had time to reflect on the worthiness of our now-defaulted commitment to the people of non-Communist South Vietnam. From the outset, we sought to help the government and armed forces of Vietnam defeat externally directed and supported Communist aggression, thus giving an independent South Vietnam a secure environment.

Historically, most wars fought in foreign lands were waged to acquire those lands as part of political or economic empires. Vietnam was an exception to that rule.

Indeed, history may judge America's experience in South Vietnam as one of man's nobler crusades—the simple desire of a strong nation to help an aspiring nation reach a point where it had a chance of achieving and keeping a degree of independence. For ten years America held the line in Vietnam against Communist expansion in Southeast Asia so that other nations could mature politically and resist future Communist pressures.

We did not fight alone in Vietnam. Thirty-four other nations contributed food, medicine, equipment, training, economic aid, and technical advisors. Four (Australia, New Zealand, Thailand, and the Republic of the Philippines) provided a civic action group with its own security force. Foreign troops totaled 68,800, more than had fought for the United Nations in Korea.

What hope is there for those who aspire to freedom if only the Communists are allowed to assist people of emerging nations? We may not be able to be the world's policeman, but neither can we neglect the responsibilities that fate gives us. If there is to be no more support of countries like Vietnam, is there to be no more support of aspiring freedom? No more protection of the weak against the strong?

Ironically, Vietnam Veterans deserve even more appreciation than their veteran counterparts of World War II and Korea. Why? Simply because in earlier wars the country was generally unified behind its men fighting in battle. But not in Vietnam.

Can you imagine putting your life on the line in the combat zone while, from a campus remote from the battlefield, a neighbor supported your armed enemy? Can you imagine living through that ordeal only to come home to stony silence and hostility? The psychological pressures on the Vietnam Veteran who had worn his country's uniform were overwhelming.

In the aftermath of Vietnam, we have heard so much about the emotionally disabled that many Americans think most Vietnam Veterans are under psychiatric care. Such is not the case. Despite the emotional scars borne by many veterans, there is little difference between the percentage of healthy Vietnam vets and veterans who returned healthy from other wars.

As I have traveled around this huge country of ours, I have met many, many Vietnam Veterans. The overwhelming majority are doing very well indeed. They are a valuable national asset, and they are moving into positions of responsibility and leadership across the spectrum of our society.

Most Vietnam Veterans are proud, as they should be, of their military service and their efforts in Vietnam. They can be assured that it was not they who lost the war.

Thank God, the worn and tired attitudes of a decade ago are almost history. A more sensible attitude toward the Vietnam War and toward those involved has emerged. Time has begun to heal the wounds. And as truth overshadows perceptions, facts are beginning to overwhelm emotions.

Today's healthier attitude by and toward those who fought the war is made evident by: the dedication, in 1982, of the Vietnam Veterans Memorial in Washington, D.C.; the Memorial's rededication, including the soldier statue, in 1984; and the official and public recognition and burial of the Unknown Soldier.

Indeed, the citizens of our nation have maintained our traditional values — values that have contributed in a major way to the character and success of the United States of America.

Gen. William C. Westmoreland, U.S. Army (Ret.) is former commander of U.S. forces in Vietnam.

PAUL B SEVERLOH · JAMES L STEINEKE · JOE F KELLEY · JAMES E THOMAS Jr ·
CHARLES M TITUS · RUSSELL M WAGNER · JAMES L WATKINS · VINCENT J WEEDO Jr ·
JOHN F BERGERSON · LARRY W BIEDIGER · JOHN J SHAW · JOHN I COOK ·
CHARLES E FAGGETT · PERRY L HARRIS · ALFRED B MAY · LYNN L MILES ·
FREDERICK M BONANNO · CLAUDE A SILVA · DONALD S SULLIVAN ·
GARY E WARD · CHARLES ESTERS Jr · RICHARD GARCIA · PAUL D HOLLOWAY ·
DANIEL J MYERS · RICHARD L PARHAM · ROBERT L POSEY Jr · RUDOLPH REMULAR ·
HOWARD L BARDEN · DAVID D BERKHOLZ · GARY E BULLOCK ·
EDWARD P HANSHAW · MICHAEL T JONES · ROY R KUBLEY ·
HARVEY MULHAUSER · ERNEST T DUPONT · WILLIAM H STRAUGHN ·
MERRILL V BEASLEY · WILLIAM A BEYER · JOHN C BOHANNON ·
WALTER R DALEY · DAVID J FRISCHMANN · JAMES D HENDERSON ·
ROBERT W MARTIN · JAMES P McGRATH · RICHARD P McSTRAVICK Jr ·
WILLARD A PHILSON · ROBERT J PRAZINKO · JERRY D WORTHY ·
WILLIAM D SCHADDELEE · JOHN H WELCH III · LEONARD ROBINSON Jr ·
JOE R FULGHUM Jr · ROGER D HERRANDO ·
EDWARD F MANNS · THOMAS M MARTINEZ · LUIS G MORA ·
MARION G RUNION · LARRY E SMITH · LARRY E SMITH ·
HAROLD E BERG Jr ·
ADAM FISCHER · JAMES E FORSMAN ·
HAROLD E LEE ·
PHILIP J SMITH ·
ROGER B TIERNBERG ·
RONALD C KISSINGER · HERB DOBY ·
WILLIAM C ENGEBRETSON ·
CHARLES E HASSLER Jr ·
KENNETH F UNDERWOOD ·
DAVID T BELL ·
GEORGE E BYRD ·
THEODORE H DAVIS ·
FELICISIMO A HUGO ·
MICHAEL J LUTZKE ·
CALVIN C MORGAN ·
MATTHEW T ORTON ·
CLARENCE H RICKARDS ·
RICHARD I STERLING ·
GEORGE T VOELMAR ·
ROBERT C ALLEN · HAROLD J ·
WILSON L COOK · JESUS ROSAS ·
GARY L FULLER · SANTIAGO RODRI ·
LITCHFIELD P HUIE · JOHN W JACKS ·
JOSE R LOZANO · SAMMY E MONRO ·
ROLAND W RAY · GEORGE ROWLAN ·
OTIS B SINK ·
CONRAD F STRAUB ·
CLARENCE VARNADO ·
JOHN C AGEE ·

FOREWORD BY

James Quay

I first went to the Wall in February 1984 during my first visit to Washington, D.C., in nearly 15 years. I had heard about the Vietnam Veterans Memorial, had seen photographs and film of it, and knew what an emotional impact it had on visitors.

As I walked along Constitution Avenue toward the Memorial, I kept looking for the black granite walls made familiar by photographs. When I couldn't see them, the landscape before me on the Mall became uncanny. Somewhere ahead of me I began to feel the Memorial as a specter that I would confront abruptly. The lightness of anticipation I had been feeling became weighted with a kind of dread.

Like all too many Americans, I was coming to the Memorial with a name to look for: Glendon Waters. He wasn't my comrade-in-arms, or a friend, or a relative. In fact, we had never met. Glendon Waters had been dead over two years when, on a cold November night in 1969, I carried his name on a placard around my neck in the "March against Death."

In that march, 45,000 people, each with the name of an American killed in action in Vietnam and a lighted candle, walked across the Arlington Memorial Bridge, past the west side of the Lincoln Memorial to 1600 Pennsylvania Avenue. There each marcher paused before the main entrance of the White House, stepped on a short wooden stand, and, one by one, said the name he or she carried, loudly or softly as they chose. It took nearly 40 hours to say all the names.

In November 1982 the names were spoken again in the Candlelight Vigil of Names that preceded the dedication of the Vietnam Veterans Memorial. This time the names weren't being shouted at the White House but were being intoned quietly in the National Cathedral. And this time it wasn't the war's opponents who spoke the names, but the war's veterans. Yet the spirit was the same. As we had once shouted the names to demonstrate that the war's individual costs were not to be forgotten, now the war's veterans were intoning the names, for the very same reason.

Suddenly, I turned a corner and there they were. There they were, all the names. They started at ground level and rose slowly as I walked down the path, rose until I felt I was descending into an open grave. At the center I stopped, in the midst of the names that now towered over me, closed my eyes, bowed my head, and just stood there, utterly overwhelmed. There are so very many names.

The names receded only when I walked up the path to the directory. Glendon Lee Waters: panel 23 East, line 33. Back down into the Memorial, I found the name of the man who had been killed just as I had publicly begun to oppose the war. What would we have said to one another if we'd met then in July of 1967? Or now? What would we say to one another now?

The Memorial makes meetings possible between the living and the dead. Some of these meetings are depicted in this book. Here, children meet fathers they never knew. Parents meet sons. Lovers are reunited. Comrades. Glendon Waters and me.

The names of the dead wait here for the living to come close and touch them. But as the Wall gives them to us, it also takes them away again, for touching the names only makes us feel how far away they are. They must remain there, united by their shared catastrophe, while we, the living, must leave, united by our shared grief.

It was this grief that made me climb the steps of another Memorial to gaze at the somber face of Abraham Lincoln. That face had known grief, and I felt that Lincoln, of all Americans living or dead, would understand what I was feeling. He too looks upon the Wall. Only when I read again the words he had used to heal a divided nation—"With malice toward none, with charity for all"—did I feel my pilgrimage was complete.

I am profoundly grateful to the dedicated men and women who built the Memorial, for they have given all who were hurt by the Vietnam War the shrine we need if we are ever to be healed. Like the war it recalls, the Memorial has been denounced and defended. But, like this book, it brings together the conscientious objector and the general, the protestor and the warrior. Important differences between us may remain, but the Memorial has given us something still more important—the common ground of grief. So long as such grief is heartfelt, shared, and remembered—always—there is hope for peace, and so for us all.

The generations wounded by the war will come to the Wall, bringing our scars and our memories with us, looking for healing. But to truly heal ourselves, we must ensure that when future generations look upon the Memorial, they will not have lost what we have lost to feel the absolute, silent sorrow embodied by the black walls, the American names that are on them, and the Vietnamese names that are not.

James Quay is a Conscientious Objector from the Vietnam War era. He is Executive Director of the California Council for the Humanities.

THOMAS C ELDRIDGE · JOSEPH P FANN
· BRUCE B GREENE · CHARLES F GRIFFIN · JAMES C
McCLENDON · FRANCIS J McGOULDRICK Jr · EDD
· DONALD A PETTITT · DAVID W PIERCE · SALVAT
AMMY RAY PALMER · ROY STOWE · WILLIAM E VAN

D A BROWN · NEIL R BURNHAM · RAMON CASTRO-
KENNETH R CRIST · RICHARD G DRAKE · RICHARD
MES R HAMMERSLA · JOHN R HARTKEMEYER · JOH
M KUPIEC · ROBERT R MASCARENAS · GEORGE W M
CE F SIMPKIN · MORTON H SINGER · FRANK N SMIT
· ROGER H STROUT · GERALD J SZOSZOREK · GEO
GER A BROWN · NORMAN H CLARK · MANCOL R C
· JOHN J GOTT Jr · RONALD L HOVIS · DONALD
Y I BARRAS · KENNETH B MILLHOUSE · ROGER C M

INTRODUCTION
The Vietnam Veterans Memorial

Vietnam. That single word still conjures up a wide range of emotions among adult Americans. The Vietnam War was the longest in our nation's history—July 1957 to May 1975. And except for the Civil War, which pitted brother against brother, it was the most divisive.

Nearly 2.7 million Americans served in the war zone. Of that number, close to 60,000 men and women were killed; 300,000 were wounded; and 75,000 were permanently disabled. And still there are almost 2,500 persons listed as "missing in action."

For many Americans, simple mention of places such as Khe Sanh, Ia Drang, A Shau, Saigon, Danang, Quang Tri, Can Tho, and An Loc can bring to mind memories of battles fought and friends lost, momentary triumphs and long-term losses. The sights, sounds, smells, and heat of Vietnam are imprinted in the minds of all who served there.

Vietnam was another world. Another life. It was difficult to explain to those back home in America. Many veterans did not discuss their experiences in Vietnam until the creation of the Vietnam Veterans Memorial.

In earlier wars, groups of soldiers who came home together had been welcomed by supporting crowds. But during the Vietnam War, America was divided. And the 365-day tour— 395 for Marines—meant that few of those who survived that year received any home-front recognition. And few of those who died were publicly mourned until the creation of the Vietnam Veterans Memorial.

A small group of Vietnam Veterans, led by Jan C. Scruggs, John P. Wheeler III, Robert Doubek, and Sandie Fauriol, wanted their fellow Americans to remember the service and sacrifice of their compatriots. Because of their perseverance, the Vietnam Veterans Memorial, with its nearly 60,000 names, stands today on the Mall in Washington, D.C. The Memorial is a lasting remembrance of the American men and women who gave their lives, and of those who remain missing in action, as the result of the Vietnam War. This black granite wall also commemorates those who served and then returned to live and work in America.

Historians have noted that participation in a war is often a watershed event in people's lives. The war in Vietnam had this effect upon the generation that came of age in the 1960s. Barring another major crisis, the war will continue to influence the lives of almost 60 million Americans.

As John Wheeler, Chair of the Vietnam Veterans Memorial Fund, has noted, among the Vietnam generation "the war separated the man who wore the uniform from the man who did not." At home, those who actively opposed American support of South Vietnam often shunned those who served. And Vietnam vets criticized those who protested the war.

Many people viewed the Vietnam Veterans Memorial as the first step in healing some of the divisions that had occurred during the war. As Wheeler has written, "The war created or magnified deep separations [that] will hurt our national life unless we take conscious steps for healing."

Just as the war generated a variety of reactions among Americans, the Vietnam Veterans Memorial has meant different things to the people who participated in the three major events photographically documented here. But all who have visited the Wall have been moved by the experience.

When the Vietnam Veterans Memorial was under construction, the staff of the Smithsonian Institution's Office of Printing and Photographic Services decided to photograph major events relating to the Memorial. This activity was part of an ongoing project instituted in 1976 by the office's director, James H. Wallace, Jr., to create a permanent photographic record of significant events occurring on or near the Mall in the nation's capital.

The five days of events of the November 1982 National Salute to Vietnam Veterans were photographed by a team of four Smithsonian photographers. Each day, from dawn until long into the night, this team recorded hundreds of images. Over the past four years, these same individuals, supported by some part-time photographers and interns, have continued to document activities at the Wall. Their work has been supplemented by colleagues and interns working with the Office of Printing and Photographic Services. The power of many of the images they recorded is clearly evident in the following pages.

No one—politician or photographer, veteran or historian—knew what to expect at the National Salute to Vietnam Veterans. No one could predict the tone of events. How would people react to the Memorial? Would there be self-congratulation or self-criticism? Would old animosities between wartime hawks and doves be rekindled, or would the events bring the nation together? The uncertainty led many national political leaders to stay away from that first event at the Wall. And it increased the importance of documenting and recording the event.

Many Washington-based observers, especially the Smithsonian photographers, soon realized that the National Salute was just the first in a series of dynamic events that would unfold at the Memorial site. The Smithsonian team continued to record the events as they evolved. In May 1984, there was the burial of the Unknown Soldier from the Vietnam War. At that solemn event, the national leadership, led by the President and members of Congress, participated in full force. By so doing, they contributed greatly to the healing process. In November 1984, there was the dedication of the soldier statue, a long-demanded addition to the Memorial site.

At each of these events, there were formal, official activities and there were personal activities, including specific rituals. First, individuals searched the Wall for names. Ex-GIs looked for former comrades. Parents, spouses, and children looked for the names of loved ones.

Later came the phenomenon of placing Vietnam-era mementos—hats, flags, pictures, boots—at the Memorial wall. At the dedication of the soldier statue, visitors also began to leave souvenirs at the feet of the bronze soldiers. But many people seemed in need of a remembrance to take home. After finding the names of lost friends or loved ones, they made pencil rubbings of them.

The final pages of this volume illustrate the continuing attraction of the Vietnam Veterans Memorial for the nation. The Memorial remains a focal point for Americans who were touched by the war and are still trying to come to grips with its meaning.

This book of photographs has been gathered together to aid documentation of the human experience at the Wall. It is offered as a small contribution to the national need to understand the significance of the American experience in the war that happened so far away.

Reflections on the Wall is dedicated to all who served their country when called upon to do so. It is also dedicated to those who lost someone over there.

EDWARD CLINTON EZELL

CEREMONIES
Events and the Wall

Ceremonies—large or small, public or private—allow human beings to express emotions that might otherwise remain bottled up.

Ceremonies are an essential element of our lives, especially when they enable us to come to grips with strong emotions, such as grieving.

The ceremonies associated with the loss of friends and loved ones in Vietnam were often delayed because of uncertainty about the effect they would have on the survivors and on the nation. And ceremonies celebrating the homecomings of Vietnam Veterans were postponed for similar reasons.

Much of that reticence changed with the dedication of the Vietnam Veterans Memorial. People came to the Memorial and found its presence heartening, even in moments of deep sadness.

Since the dedication of the Memorial in November 1982, the polished black granite wall has become the focal point for numerous ceremonies, public and private. The Wall has provided veterans with a gathering place—a place to remember those who served, those who were wounded, those who died, those who remain unaccounted for. Public or private, mournful or joyous, these Memorial-centered ceremonies have become part of the post–Vietnam War healing process.

Once the ceremonies began to unfold in the fall of 1982, it quickly became evident that time had started to blunt some of the conflicts that existed between the war's supporters and its opponents, between the participants and the nonparticipants.

Reconciliation and healing are far from complete, but the Vietnam Veterans Memorial has served a cathartic role for many Americans. It has allowed them to place the Vietnam years in perspective and to move on with the rest of their lives.

Ceremonies surrounding the Vietnam Veterans
Memorial began with the five-day National Salute to
Vietnam Veterans, November 10–14, 1982.

They began at the National Cathedral with a solemn
56-hour event during which 250 volunteers took
turns reading the names of every man and woman
whose name appears on the walls of the Memorial.
As a continuing reminder of sacrifices made by
those who did not return from Vietnam, an
around-the-clock vigil was maintained at the
National Cathedral for the remainder of the week's
activities.

Above: David DeChant and Sandie Fauriol began the
reading of the names.

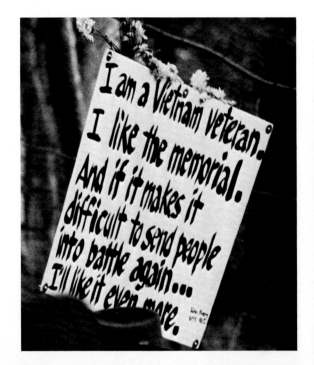

People came from all over the United States to participate in the November 1982 National Salute to Vietnam Veterans, including the parade down Constitution Avenue. Some came with only their sleeping bags and camping gear. Having no other place to stay, they slept on the lawn in front of the Vietnam Veterans Memorial. Of those in this unofficial bivouac, many subsisted on combat rations. In keeping with the spirit of the Salute, and despite their unauthorized presence, these fresh-air vets were not disturbed by police or National Park Service personnel.

Many Gold Star mothers, women who have lost sons in this nation's wars, participated in the November 1982 National Salute to Vietnam Veterans. These mothers were strong and emotional supporters of the Vietnam Veterans who gathered in the nation's capital for the Salute's events.

At the time of the 1982 National Salute to Vietnam Veterans, the federal government had yet to decide about a burial service and tomb for the Unknown Soldier from the Vietnam War. Several marchers in the parade pleaded for recognition of the soldier known only to God. Not until Memorial Day 1984 were their pleas answered.

The November 13 parade down Washington's Constitution Avenue was the first large-scale public event of the 1982 National Salute to Vietnam Veterans.

Organized alphabetically by state delegations, the parade was led by an assortment of grand marshalls and other VIPs. Alabama, the first state in the parade, had half-a-dozen Vietnam vets present.

Moments before the parade began, Retired General William C. Westmoreland, who had been sitting in the reviewing stand, learned that the Vietnam Veterans themselves were going to march and decided to march with them. Westmoreland left the stand and joined the Alabama contingent to lead the parade.

The parade was a gathering of former comrades in honor of fallen or missing comrades. It mattered not that there once was disagreement in the ranks about the war and its goals. The war was past, and these veterans were officially coming home.

During the parade and subsequent ceremonies, it was clear that General Westmoreland was much respected by the Vietnam Veterans because of his spontaneous and personal participation in the activities at the Memorial. For some vets, General Westmoreland was simply their former commander. For others, he symbolized their struggle for recognition and acceptance. But all appreciated his presence at the events celebrating the Vietnam Veterans Memorial.

Organizers estimate 150,000 people gathered for the dedication of the Vietnam Veterans Memorial. The size of this crowd surprised even most of the people who had labored to bring about the events.

The dedication of the Vietnam Veterans Memorial culminated four years of intense activity. Building the Memorial required the commitment of a small cadre of dedicated leaders and the assistance of a small army of volunteers.

The Memorial was the idea of Jan C. Scruggs (*left*). Scruggs was supported in his quest to raise money and to garner political support for the Vietnam Veterans Memorial by Robert W. Doubek, John P. Wheeler III, and Sandie Fauriol (*above left*). Few in number at the outset, the political supporters of the project included Senator John W. Warner from Virginia (*above right*), who spoke at the November 1982 dedication ceremonies.

Most Vietnam Veterans who came to the 1982 dedication came alone. They reflected upon the Memorial as individuals. They reminisced with former comrades about their war. Coming to the Memorial was an intense personal experience. And many still felt a sense of separation.

Most political or military leaders chose to stay away from the 1982 activities. The homecoming process was still incomplete. Only staunch supporters of the Vietnam Veterans Memorial, such as Senators John W. Warner and Charles McC. Mathias were there, as was

Retired General William C. Westmoreland.

In 1984, although the crowd was smaller, the Vietnam Veterans brought their spouses and children in a second phase of the homecoming process. While far from solving all the problems, it was obvious that the Vietnam Veterans Memorial and its soldier statue served as a catalyst in the healing process.

The Veterans Day 1984 rededication of the Vietnam Veterans Memorial saw full participation of the nation's political leadership. In addition to the Vietnam Veterans Memorial Foundation staff and other prominent individ-

uals who had been present during the 1982 ceremonies, President Ronald Reagan and First Lady Nancy Reagan, Defense Secretary Caspar W. Weinberger, and other national leaders formally welcomed the veterans of the Vietnam War back home.

There was a sense of community as veterans, families, and other Americans began to share the experience of reflecting on the Wall. People began to take pencil rubbings from the names on the Wall.

Sculptor Frederick Hart described his statue of American infantrymen: "The portrayal of the figures is consistent with history. They wear the uniform and carry the equipment of war; they are young. The contrast between the innocence of their youth and the weapons of war underscores the poignancy of their sacrifice. There is about them the physical contact and sense of unity that bespeaks the bonds of love and sacrifices that are the nature of men at war. And yet they are each alone. Their strength and their vulnerability are both evident. Their true heroism lies in these bonds of loyalty in the face of their aloneness and their vulnerability."

The base of the soldier statue has become an altar upon which Vietnam Veterans have left wartime objects — Zippo lighters, patches, campaign ribbons, flags, dog tags, P38 can openers, C-rations, full cans of beer, Holy Bibles and other books, such as the Bhagavad Gita. All of these items represent "good-stuff," not trash. They are, in effect, devotional offerings laid at the feet of the Vietnam-era infantryman. Because of the historical importance of the memorabilia, the National Park Service has been collecting and preserving it.

Joe Ambrose, a World War I veteran from Joliet, Illinois, wore his classic, but tattered, World War I uniform. He came to Washington to participate in the National Salute to Vietnam Veterans.

Joe had lost a son in the Korean War. Clutching the neatly folded American flag that he had received at his son's funeral, Joe was obviously proud to be at the Memorial site.

Those gathered at the Memorial, especially the Vietnam Veterans, took a special liking to Joe Ambrose. The crowd gently pushed him forward toward the "snow fence" that separated them all from the Memorial itself. Then to calls of "Let Joe through!" they raised him on their shoulders, while he proudly held the flag over his head.

The police had little choice but to help Joe over the fence. To the cheers of the people assembled at the Memorial, he saluted the younger veterans. Afterward, he lingered and chatted with as many of the Vietnam Veterans as he could. Between these representatives of two distinctive generations, there was the bond of individuals who have seen combat in a foreign land.

REFLECTING ON THE WALL
The Search for Friends

People from all over the nation came to the dedication of the Vietnam Veterans Memorial. And since that time, for a variety of reasons, they have continued to visit the Memorial in large numbers. Perhaps one of the most common motivations has been to search for the names of friends, comrades, loved ones—names that are recorded for posterity on the black granite walls.

Parents, spouses, children, friends, and strangers come to the Vietnam Veterans Memorial. Most seek to find only a name or two among the nearly 60,000 names of Americans who died, or who are still unaccounted for, in this nation's longest war. But the presence of all the names seldom softens the blow of finding the one name—the special name—of one specific and special person who was lost.

Searching for a single name is complicated by the fact that the names are listed chronologically, in the order that the people whom they represent became casualties. The decision to list the names this way was controversial during the planning of the Memorial. A chronological listing is not as neat and orderly as an alphabetical one. But the emotional impact of the Memorial is greater than it would have been with an alphabetical listing.

The position of a name on the Wall tells a story. It fixes a death or a disappearance at a specific point in time. There are clumps of names representing men who died in the same ambush, or individuals who died together in a helicopter crash. There are the names of lone pilots who were shot down over North Vietnam. There are the names of nurses who died when their hospitals came under enemy attack. The names recount the pace and tempo of the war.

People search the names. People contemplate the names. People touch the names. And by 1984, people began to take pencil rubbings from the names on the Memorial's walls.

There seems to be nearly a universal need to come into contact with the letters engraved on the stone panels. The letters that compose a name. The letters that record a life. The letters that tell of a death.

Coming to the Memorial and searching its walls has in many ways created a sense of community among visitors. Those who come in search of a name know that for all time the person who had that name has been lost to the living because of the war in Vietnam.

Because the names are listed chronologically on the Vietnam Veterans Memorial, the National Park Service has provided a directory and volunteers to aid visitors in their search.

As this woman searched for the name of her son, who died early in the war, an airplane headed for Washington's National Airport was reflected on the polished surface of the Wall. *Facing page:* She wore her son's Distinguished Flying Cross, Air Medals (with three oak-leaf clusters), and his Purple Heart when she visited the Memorial.

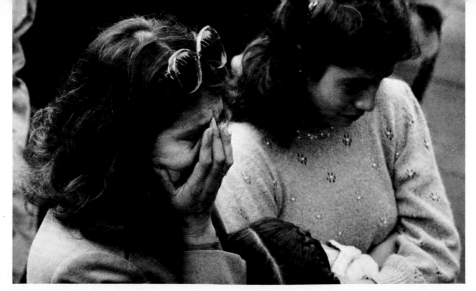

Man, woman, and child. Few who have visited the Vietnam Veterans Memorial and have found the name they were seeking have come away unmoved by the experience. Many have spoken of the feeling of necessity, as well as the courage required to look for a name on the Memorial's walls.

Taking rubbings from the memorials of fallen
warriors and individuals of note is an age-long
tradition that continues at the Vietnam Veterans
Memorial. By 1984, people spontaneously had
begun to take pencil and crayon rubbings from the
names on the Memorial's walls. Most frequently,
they recorded the name on the National Park
Service brochure that was handed out at the site.
Men and women of all ages and ethnic backgrounds
paused to record the name of that special one who
had been lost.

GATHERING AT THE WALL
Remembering the Vietnam Experience

The Vietnam Veterans Memorial has become a major tourist attraction in the nation's capital. Visiting the Memorial is on the "must" list of things to do.

During the years since the 1982 dedication of the Vietnam Veterans Memorial, there have been many major gatherings at the Memorial site. While some people prefer to come to the Memorial alone or as part of a very small group, others come to participate in the larger official and unofficial gatherings. They come to the Memorial with a variety of personal goals and motivations.

Some simply want to be where their fellow soldiers are remembered. They know that comradeship does not cease with the death of a friend. Survivors feel an obligation to those lost to keep their memory alive.

Others want to be there where their loved ones are memorialized—youngsters lost forever, but never forgotten.

Some visit the Memorial to reflect on the past—their past. Vietnam's war and its impact on their lives have left indelible memories.

Some seek answers. They still need to come to grips with their lives. As a result of losing friends or loved ones, they still have readjustments to make.

The most common questions start with a single word—Why? Many know that, except for some curious twist of fate, their name could have been on the Wall. Others have asked, "Why am I here now, no longer young, with even fewer answers than I had then?"

The walls of the Vietnam Veterans Memorial provide visitors with a psychological shelter where they can ask such painful and searching questions without fearing that others will rebuke or reprove them. The Memorial has contributed to bringing Vietnam Veterans and those who remained at home closer together again.

Many veterans who visit the Vietnam Veterans Memorial still show the physical scars of combat. But many of them count themselves among the fortunate ones as they contemplate the names of those who did not come home from Southeast Asia.

HAROLD

ALLAN G SWAIM · WI

JOS

RONALD C BAKEWE

WILLIAM

CARL L GE

EDWARD M MAHE

IN MEMORIAM

Pfc. Ronald C. "Smokey" Bakewell

Precious thoughts, silent tears
loving memories of our son and
brother, who was killed in action
in Vietnam, 14 years ago today,
August 2, 1968.
  Years may pass and seasons
change
  But time cannot erase
  The special talks, the happy
times
  The smile upon your face.
  You gave to us many special
gifts
  Not tied with ribbon and bow
  But thoughts shared and
lessons learned
  That's why we miss you so.
  Sunshine fades and shadows
fall
  But sweet remembrance
outlast them all.
  Our lips cannot tell how much
we miss you.
  Our hearts cannot tell what to
say.
  You alone know how much we
miss you
  in a home that is sometimes
lonely today.

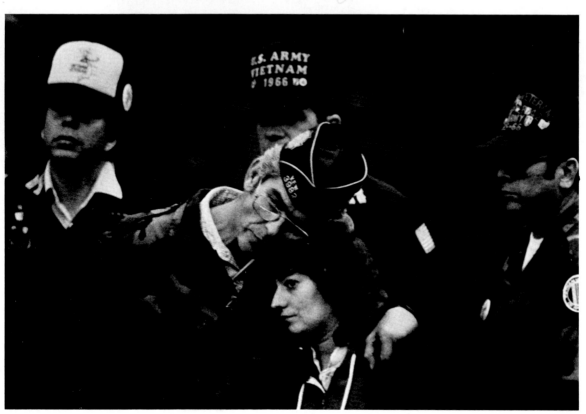

A lone veteran watched the dedication of the Memorial from the isolation of a nearby tree. The American flag was held by one of the thousands of spectators below.

Vietnam amputee, Bob Wieland, stood in his
wheelchair as he talked with his fellow vets.

Some reunions at the Vietnam Veterans Memorial have been joyful occasions.

Tommy Roubideaux, a Sioux Indian from South Dakota, was a Special Forces medic in Vietnam. Chuck Woolf, a Deputy Sheriff from Ohio, served in the same 101st Airborne unit as Roubideaux. The two men became very close friends during the year they served together.

Then one day in 1967, Woolf was wounded several times during a special mission. Before he was evacuated by helicopter, Roubideaux stabilized his condition.

Later, Roubideaux heard that Woolf had died after arriving at the Evac hospital. When Woolf learned that only 8 men from his group of 25 had survived, he concluded, in turn, that Roubideaux had been killed.

During the November 1982 dedication of the Vietnam Veterans Memorial, both Tommy Roubideaux and Chuck Woolf went to the Wall, each looking for the other's name. Instead, they found each other alive and well.

Sadness turned to joy. Roubideaux was so moved by his reunion with Woolf that he petitioned to have him adopted as a warrior in the Sioux tribe. In 1984, the petition was granted, and Woolf's induction began with the Eagle Feather ceremony at the Wall, which is recorded here.

While Woolf will not become a Sioux warrior for several more years, the Sioux have already accepted him as a brother and as a son.

There were other happy reunions at the events surrounding the ceremonies at the Vietnam Veterans Memorial . . .

REUNIONS
Meeting Friends, Old and New

Although there were bad times and suffering associated with the war in Southeast Asia, there were some good times as well. The same was true of the reunions scheduled during the events at the Vietnam Veterans Memorial. These events brought individuals together after as many as 15 or 20 years. Because the military experience in Southeast Asia had been unique, these Vietnam-related gatherings were more intense than any high school or college reunion.

Old friendships were renewed. New friendships were started. Men and women who had served together, and individuals who had never met before—but who had the common experience of having lived, fought, and survived in 'Nam—came together in celebration.

Smiles and tears, handshakes and hugs, and war stories abounded. Whiskey and beer flowed just as it had "in-country" years before. Many veterans took photographs and exchanged addresses.

But much more important, they talked. So much had been unsaid for so long. Conversations—humorous, sad, casual, intense—lasted all night and on into the new day. As memories flooded back, veterans recalled times past—both good and bad. And while they remembered those who had been lost, they gave thanks for all those who had survived Vietnam.

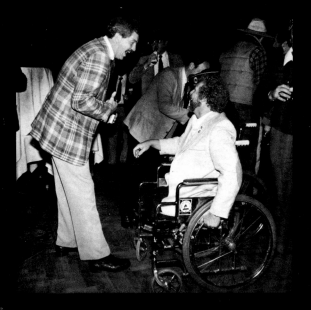

There were still friends who were missing. Some veterans spent their time searching the names on the Wall and the faces in the crowd for those whose fate they did not know. Throughout the events at the Vietnam Veterans Memorial there was overwhelming concern for the remaining MIAs and POWs.

FOUNDATION
LITY OF POW/MIAs
ANYONE RECOGNIZE
THIS MAN?
PLEASE CALL
JIM MANN
483-2000
ROOM 107
I've been carrying this Picture for 17 yrs - can't Remember name
Radio Operator
B Co 1/327th
101st Abn V.N.
1966-67

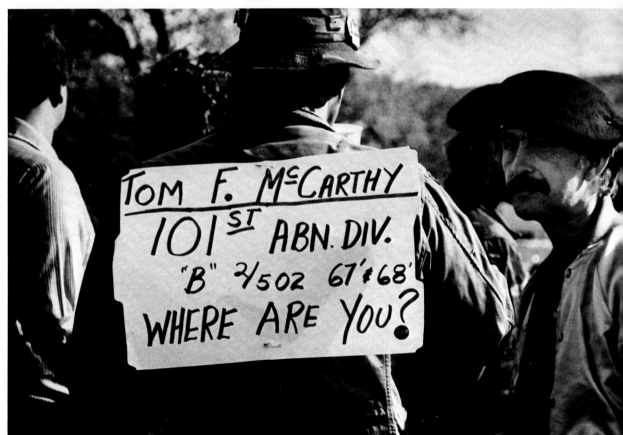

One path to survival in Vietnam was the "Party." The reunions also had their share of parties where the Vietnam Veterans enjoyed themselves at their delayed homecoming celebration. At one party, "Wolfman Jack," the best-known Vietnam-era disc jockey, poured drinks for men who had listened to his broadcasts a long time ago in a land far away.

During the 1984 dedication of the soldier statue there was a spontaneous movement for an event in which all visitors could participate. This movement grew out of the belief of POW groups, especially among the children of POWs, that there was a need for a grass-roots activity. The result was the candlelight ceremony at the Vietnam Veterans Memorial.

The beauty of thousands of flickering candles made this event one of the most memorable in a series of moving activities. Once again the outpouring of human emotion at the Memorial illustrated how deeply the Vietnam War had touched many lives.

UNFINISHED BUSINESS
The Continuing Impact of Vietnam

On Friday, November 12, 1982, the Vietnam Veterans of America organized two forums at which their wartime comrades could discuss issues of intense personal concern.

One forum involved the long-term biological effects of the herbicide "Agent Orange." Between 1962 and 1970, in an attempt to deny the enemy the concealment offered by the jungle and the woodland foliage, U.S. armed forces sprayed 10.6 million gallons of Agent Orange over remote regions of South Vietnam.

Originally, this herbicide was believed to be of limited threat to the health of humans. Now, unusual levels of life-threatening disorders, such as cancer, have begun to manifest themselves among Vietnam Veterans. And birth defects and other genetic disorders have begun to appear in their children. As a result, an ongoing debate rages among veteran and government organizations.

The other group of discussions centered on the subsequent psychological disorders experienced by Vietnam-era veterans. These problems are generally grouped under the term "post-traumatic stress disorder"—a catchall phrase that covers a variety of psychological and personal adjustment problems that have affected veterans of the Vietnam War.

Generally, troublesome flashbacks and related problems have cropped up years after the individual returned from the war. Many veterans have had difficulty adjusting to the peacetime environment after their combat experiences. Work habits have been affected, marriages destabilized, families jeopardized. Debilitating for some, these post-traumatic stress problems have been worrisome for others as they have tried to proceed with their lives.

The November 12 forums gave veterans who had previously been unable to have their say an opportunity to express their thoughts, fears, and emotions about both Agent Orange and post-traumatic stress disorders.

THE UNKNOWN
A Vietnam Soldier Returns

On Memorial Day 1984, after lying in state in the Capitol rotunda, the remains of an unknown American soldier of the Vietnam War were laid to rest at Arlington National Cemetery. His identity "known only to God," the Unknown Soldier, officially known as the Unknown Serviceman, is entombed beside the Unknowns of World Wars I and II and the Korean War.

By virtue of this ceremony, this soldier became the representative of all who had died or who were still unaccounted for in Southeast Asia. The President, members of Congress, and other senior government officials participated in events surrounding the funeral and burial of the Vietnam War Unknown Soldier.

Of all the personal losses of loved ones suffered during war, one of the most wrenching is accompanied by the words "Missing in Action." Because of the unresolved status of the nearly 2,500 Americans still listed as MIA from the Vietnam War, the funeral and burial of the Unknown Soldier was extremely poignant for many families. The ceremony was a reminder of the work that remains to be done in resolving the fate of the MIAs.

Interment of the Vietnam War Unknown Soldier officially brought an end to an era. But for many families, the Vietnam War will be unfinished as long as there are people listed as MIA and an Unknown Soldier.

As the cortege for the Unknown Soldier made its way down Constitution Avenue and Bacon Drive, it passed the Vietnam Veterans Memorial. Ever so briefly, the color guard paused and did a left-face to face the Memorial. Then, just as swiftly, they did a right-face and continued the march to Arlington Cemetery.

As part of the funeral ceremony honoring the Vietnam War Unknown Soldier, honorary pallbearers carried the casket to the amphitheater in Arlington Cemetery. There, the President and the Secretary of Defense presented the symbolic Medal of Honor.

138

At Arlington Cemetery, President Reagan received the flag from the casket of the Vietnam War Unknown Soldier. In this ceremony the President acted as the next of kin.

After the burial service for the Vietnam War
Unknown Soldier, Vietnam Veterans and other
members of the public came to pay homage to this
one "known only to God."

EPILOGUE
Continuing Events at the Wall

The official events of 1982 and 1984 were not the only events to be held at the Vietnam Veterans Memorial, nor were they the last activities.

Ceremonies—large and small—continue at the Memorial. Anniversaries of events, such as the tenth anniversary of the Fall of Saigon, have been remembered at the Memorial. In May 1986, a ceremony was held recognizing the addition of 110 more names of deceased Americans.

But, mostly, the real "life" of the Vietnam Veterans Memorial continues to consist of private ceremonies conducted quietly by individuals for whom the black granite wall still serves as a healing stone. These private reflections and remembrances give significance to the Memorial.

In 1986, a visitor left a high school 20-year reunion program at the Memorial. That person had saved the program for two years before bringing it to Washington and laying it at the Wall in memory of a fallen graduate.

Many others leave tokens of remembrance at the Memorial and at the soldier statue. And it seems likely that the Memorial will continue to play a significant role in healing a generation and the nation in which it lives.

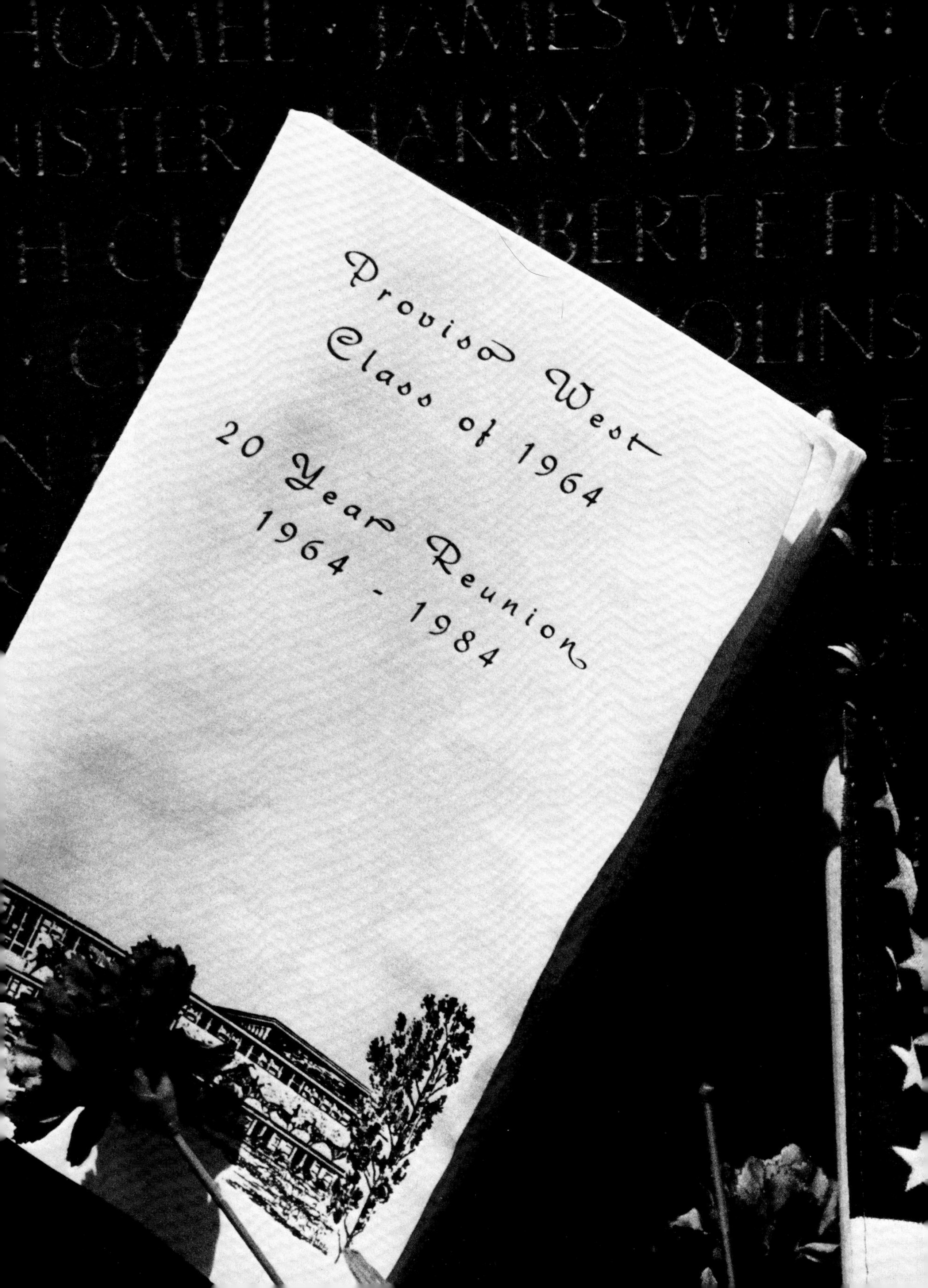

Proviso West
Class of 1964

20 Year Reunion
1964 - 1984

Bob Wieland lost his legs while serving in the 25th Infantry Division as a combat medic. He received his injuries while detonating a booby trap. Wieland gained national notice for his Knott's Berry Farm, California, to Washington, D.C., "walk" across the country on his hands, which he undertook to raise money for the hungry. He arrived at the Vietnam Veterans Memorial after a journey that took three years, eight months, and six days.

The Veteran's Vigil Society, which has been lobbying for greater visibility for the POW-MIA issue, set up their table and tent in 1982 at the time of the dedication of the Vietnam Veterans Memorial. The continued presence of their representatives camping out on the grounds of the Memorial is technically a violation of the National Park Service regulations, but no one has attempted to remove these concerned individuals. The Veteran's Vigil Society intends to remain encamped until all POWs-MIAs have been returned or have been accounted for.

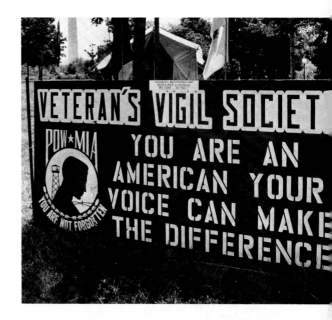

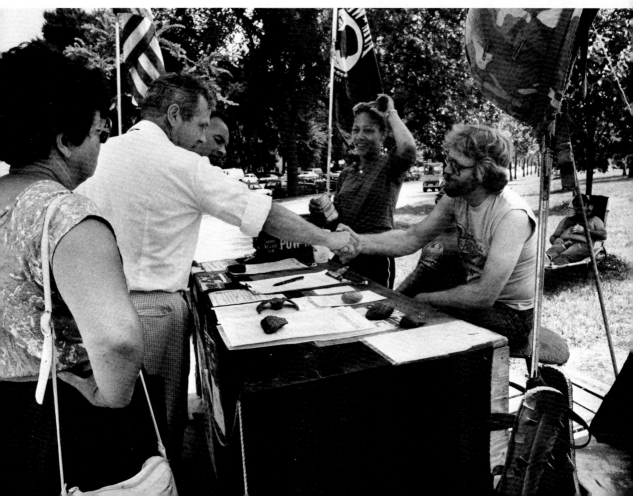

On Memorial Day 1986, the names of 110 servicemembers who died during the Vietnam War were added to the walls of the Vietnam Veterans Memorial. These names previously had been left off the Memorial because these people died outside the combat zone designated by presidential decree to include Vietnam, Cambodia, and adjacent waters. As the result of lobbying by family members and veterans' organizations, the Defense Department's new definition adds "any deaths which occurred as a result of aircraft accidents en route or return from a direct combat mission to bomb, strafe or perform surveillance of targets within the defined combat area."

As part of its support of activities at the Vietnam Veterans Memorial, in 1986, the National Park Service began providing a card that can be used for taking rubbings of names from the walls of the Memorial. At the top right it reads: "In honor of the men and women of the Armed Forces of the United States who served in the Vietnam War. The names of those who gave their lives and of those who remain missing are inscribed in the order they were taken from us." At the bottom left it says: "Our nation honors the courage, sacrifice, and devotion to duty and country of its Vietnam veterans. This Memorial was built with private contributions from the American people. November 11, 1982." These words are inscribed on the Memorial.

In the spring of 1985, on the tenth anniversary of the Fall of Saigon, children from the organization No Greater Love remembered parents lost in the Vietnam War by placing flowers and flags at the Vietnam Veterans Memorial.

HALFORD LOGAN · JE
CARL J WOODS · VIRG
WALTER J BIENKOWSK
MICHAEL D CHWAN +
WILLIAM G MAURONI
MAUSBY E HYLEMAN
JOHN J OWAS · DONA

r · HAR
RIS + EA
DHIII

Each name on the walls of the Vietnam Veterans Memorial is followed either by a diamond (indicating a death) or by a cross (indicating missing in action). When an individual MIA is confirmed to have been killed, the cross by that name is converted to a diamond. In the event that an individual listed as MIA is confirmed to have survived, a circle, as a symbol of life, will be inscribed around the cross.

Visitors come to the Vietnam Veterans Memorial at all seasons. On Christmas Day 1982, the daughters of Terry W. Cressel visited the Memorial and left a card that said, "Merry Christmas 'Angel Daddy' . . . We love you." Many cards of a similar type and other memorabilia are left daily at the Memorial.

Photo Information

Front cover: In this multiple exposure, the faces from sculptor Frederick Hart's soldier statue at the Vietnam Veterans Memorial reflect on the names of comrades killed or missing in Vietnam. *Photo by Jeffrey Ploskonka, 86-12560/14a.*

Back cover: A father and son pause before one section of the granite wall of the Vietnam Veterans Memorial engraved with almost 60,000 names. *Photo by Richard Hofmeister, 86-12561/34.*

Page 5: In this double exposure taken during the 1982 dedication ceremonies, a member of the military honor guard stands reflected against the black granite wall of names. *Photo by Jeffrey Ploskonka, 82-13714/29.*

Page 6: Detail of names, part of Panel 13E. *Photo by Jim Wallace, 86-9910/4.*

Page 8: Aerial view of the Vietnam Veterans Memorial. *Photo by Richard Hofmeister, 86-7015/34.*

Page 11: Flag and flowers left during the 1982 dedication ceremonies. *Photo by Dane A. Penland, 82-13670/20.*

Page 12: Making a rubbing from a name on the Wall. *Photo by Dane A. Penland, 84-18158/9.*

Page 14: Boots, hat, and flags left at the Wall during the 1984 rededication. *Photo by Tracey Eller, 84-18136/27.*

Page 17: Needlework and flag left at the Wall, 1982. *Photo by Dane A. Penland, 82-13695/10.*

Page 18: A young boy lies quietly on top of the Wall during the 1984 candlelight service. *Photo by Jeffrey Ploskonka, 84-18198/3.*

Page 21: Looking east toward the Washington Monument from the Vietnam Veterans Memorial at night. *Photo by Jeff Tinsley, 84-18168/30.*

Page 22: Helicopters landing during mission in Vietnam. *U.S. Army Photo, 86-10197/3A. Background: Detail of Panel 36W. Photo by Jim Wallace, 86-12127/16.*

Page 26: Honor guard during the 1982 dedication ceremonies, looking east from the top of the Wall. *Photo by Richard Hofmeister, 82-13657/9.*

Page 28: View from the balcony at the Washington National Cathedral during the reading of the almost 60,000 names, a ceremony that opened the 1982 dedication events. *Photo by Dane A. Penland, 82-13671/11.*

Page 29: David DeChant and Sandie Fauriol read the first group of names at the Washington National Cathedral. *Photo by Dane A. Penland, 82-13677/19.*

Page 30, top: Sign held by a veteran at the 1982 dedication. *Photo by Jeff Tinsley, 82-13742/16.*

Page 30, bottom: Three Vietnam Veterans who came without any place to stay, and slept at the Memorial throughout the days of the 1982 dedication events. *Photo by Jeff Tinsley, 82-13724/33.*

Page 31, top: During the parade, members of a former unit in Vietnam run together down Washington's Constitution Avenue to express their unity. *Photo by Jeff Tinsley, 82-13735/16.*

Page 31, bottom: At the 1982 parade, spectators display family pride. *Photo by Richard Hofmeister, 82-13656/31A.*

Page 32, top: Marchers in the parade carry the POW/MIA banner. *Photo by Dane A. Penland, 82-13701/64A.*

Page 32, bottom: Vets in wheelchairs show their enthusiasm during the parade. *Photo by Dane A. Penland, 82-13700/14A.*

Page 33, top: Members of the Mississippi delegation march in the parade. *Photo by Dane A. Penland, 82-13692/20.*

Page 33, bottom: Overall view of the parade. *Photo by Jeff Tinsley, 82-13747/35A.*

Page 34: A group of vets salute as the Colors pass by. *Photo by Jeffrey Ploskonka, 82-13707/21A.*

Page 35: Flags and cheering during the parade. *Photo by Dane A. Penland, 82-13693/33.*

Page 36: A Gold Star mother cheers along the parade route and is spontaneously hugged by one of the marching veterans. *Photos by Dane A. Penland, (left) 82-13701/57A & (right) 82-13701/59A.*

Page 37: Marchers in wheelchairs cheer as they pass the reviewing stand during the parade. *Photo by Richard Hofmeister, 82-13658/23.*

Page 38, top: A marcher in the 1982 parade calls for the burial of an Unknown Soldier from Vietnam. *Photo by Dane A. Penland, 82-13697/44.*

Page 38, bottom: Veterans, some showing the effects of wounds suffered in the war, march down Washington's Constitution Avenue. *Photo by Jeffrey Ploskonka, 82-13711/49.*

Page 39: Retired General William Westmoreland (*right*), former commander of U.S. forces in Vietnam, leads the veterans down Washington's Constitution Avenue in the 1982 parade. *Photo by Richard Hofmeister, 82-13662/6.*

Page 40: General Westmoreland greets veterans on the Mall during both the 1982 and 1984 events. *Photos by Richard Hofmeister, (top) 84-13113/9 and (bottom) 82-13656/8A.*

Page 41: General Westmoreland talks with a veteran in a wheelchair in front of the soldier statue in 1984. *Photo by Dane A. Penland, 84-18163/32.*

Page 42: During the 1982 dedication ceremonies, the formal military honor guard stands on top of the Wall, while the informal honor guard, established by the veterans, maintains its position below. *Photo by Jeffrey Ploskonka, 82-13704/30.*

Page 43, top: Honor guards carrying their flags, which are reflected in the Wall. *Photo by Dane A. Penland, 82-13688/3.*

Page 43, bottom: Still carrying their state signs from the parade, veterans gather at the Wall for the 1982 dedication. *Photo by Dane A. Penland, 82-13688/17.*

Page 44, top: Part of the crowd at the Wall during the 1982 ceremonies. *Photo by Jeffrey Ploskonka, 82-13712/30.*

Page 44–45: Panoramic view of the crowd, estimated at 150,000, which attended the 1982 dedication of the Memorial. *Photo by Jeff Tinsley, 82-13752/4/5.*

Page 46: Jan C. Scruggs, founder of the Vietnam Veterans Memorial, standing at the apex of the Wall. *Photo by Dane A. Penland, 82-13676/24.*

Page 47, top left: John P. Wheeler III, chair of the Vietnam Veterans Memorial Fund, speaking at the 1982 dedication. Behind him are (left) Robert Doubek and (right) Sandie Fauriol. *Photo by Dane A. Penland, 82-13690/21.*

Page 47, top right: Senator John W. Warner speaking at the 1982 dedication. *Photo by Dane A. Penland, 82-13689/10.*

Page 47, bottom: The stand with officials for the 1982 dedication. *Photo by Dane A. Penland, 82-13691/30.*

Page 48, top: President Reagan and other government officials join officials of the Vietnam Veterans Memorial Fund during the 1984 ceremonies. *Photo by Jeff Tinsley, 84-18192/56.*

Page 48, bottom: Overall view of the 1984 dedication ceremonies. *Photo by Jeff Tinsley, 84-18189/30.*

Page 49: Detail of Frederick Hart's soldier statue, dedicated in 1984. *Photo by Jeffrey Ploskonka, 84-18204/1A.*

Page 50: The soldier statue at night. *Photo by Jeff Tinsley, 84-18175/1.*

Page 51, top: The soldier statue with memorabilia that have been left. *Photo by Sandra Rodger, 84-18121/20.*

Page 51, bottom: Detail of items left at the soldier statue, including unit insignia, signs, full cans of beer, and flags. *Photo by Jeff Tinsley, 84-18193/32.*

Page 52: World War I Veteran Joe Ambrose holds an American flag aloft as he is lifted to the shoulders of the crowd during the 1982 dedication ceremonies. *Photo by Jeffrey Ploskonka, 82-13710/25.*

Page 53: World War I Veteran Joe Ambrose talks with a Vietnam Veteran. He salutes during the 1982 dedication ceremonies. *Photos by Dane A. Penland, (top) 82-13691/9 and (bottom) 82-13689/32.*

Page 54: A woman searches for the name of a loved one on the wall of the Memorial. *Photo by Richard Hofmeister, 82-13651/28.*

Pages 56–57: A sequence as a woman finds a name on the wall of the Memorial. *Photos by Richard Hofmeister, (top) 82-13651/29, (bottom) 82-13651/30 & (right) 82-13651/36.*

Page 58, top: A visitor contemplates names on the Wall. *Photo by Dane A. Penland, 82-13687/4.*

Page 58, bottom: A National Park Service volunteer assists visitors looking up names in the directory, which shows the location of each name on the Wall. *Photo by Jeff Tinsley, 82-13728/11A.*

Page 59: A veteran holds the Wall while he searches for names. *Photo by Dane A. Penland, 84-18155/36A.*

Pages 60–61: Two men search for names on the Wall. *Photo by Jeff Tinsley, 84-18185/30.*

Page 62: A mother holds her pilot son's picture against the Wall. Above the picture is the reflection of a plane landing at Washington's National Airport. *Photo by Jeff Tinsley, 82-13731/3A.*

Page 63: Wearing her son's medals, a mother displays his photograph as she stands in front of the Wall. *Photo by Dane A. Penland, 82-13670/33.*

Page 64: A boy places flags at the Wall during the 1982 dedication. *Photo by Jeff Tinsley, 82-13727/13.*

Page 65, top: Flags and a pointing hand, reflected in the Wall. *Photo by Jeffrey Ploskonka, 84-18204/34A.*

Page 65, bottom: Visitors point to names on the Wall. *Photo by Jeff Tinsley, 82-13730/24A.*

Page 66: A boy places flowers at the base of the Wall. *Photo by Jeffrey Ploskonka, 82-13710/30.*

Page 67, top: A veteran carries a flag during his visit to the Memorial. *Photo by Jeffrey Ploskonka, 82-13715/43.*

Page 67, bottom: Signs and flowers left at the Memorial. *Photo by Jeff Tinsley, 84-18186/38.*

Pages 68–69: A mother and children react after finding a name on the Wall during the 1982 dedication. *Photo by Dane A. Penland, 82-13680/35.*

Page 70: Grief often overcomes visitors to the Wall after facing the reality of finding the name of a loved one. *(Top) Photo by Jeff Tinsley, 82-13729/29; (bottom) Photo by Jeffrey Ploskonka, 82-13713/6.*

Page 71: Two vets react to grief at the Memorial. *Photo by Dane A. Penland, 84-18158/10.*

Page 72: Two veterans at the Wall. *Photo by Jeffrey Ploskonka, 82-13712/14.*

Page 73: Visitors often take photographs of names on the Wall. *Photo by Jeff Tinsley, 82-13728/19A.*

Page 74: Hands, some disabled, are reflected on the Wall while rubbings are made of names on the Wall. *Photo by Jeff Tinsley, 84-18174/23.*

Page 75: Making a rubbing from a name on the Wall. *Photo by Jeffrey Ploskonka, 84-18201/12A.*

Page 77: Faces in the crowd at the Vietnam Veterans Memorial. *Photo by Jeffrey Ploskonka, 82-13702/17.*

Page 78: Crowds above and below the Memorial press toward the Wall during the 1982 dedication ceremonies. *Photo by Jeff Tinsley, 82-13727/3.*

Page 79: A disabled vet stares at the wall of names during the 1984 dedication. *Photo by Dane A. Penland, 84-18158/25.*

Page 80: A disabled vet balances on his crutches as he contemplates the Memorial. *Photo by Jeffrey Ploskonka, 82-13712/16.*

Page 81, top: Two American Legionnaires bow their heads as they approach the Wall. *Photo by Jeffrey Ploskonka, 82-13702/21A.*

Page 81, bottom: A flower and a cane in hand, a visitor approaches the Wall. *Photo by Richard Hofmeister, 84-18113/30.*

Page 82: A message in memory of a fallen soldier lies next to his name on the Wall. *Photo by Dane A. Penland, 82-13683/25.*

Page 83, top: A face in the crowd at the Memorial. *Photo by Jeffrey Ploskonka, 82-13711/51.*

Page 83, bottom: A couple standing on top of the Wall share a moment of silence in the midst of the crowd. *Photo by Sandra Rodger, 84-18124/21.*

Page 84, top: A couple scan the Wall as they search for a name. *Photo by Jeff Tinsley, 82-13730/11A.*

Page 84, bottom: The crowd of visitors presses toward the Wall. *Photo by Jeffrey Ploskonka, 82-13712/26.*

Page 85: Visitors to the Wall often leave objects that they have carefully saved for years, such as this Teddy Bear who lost his best friend in Vietnam. *Photo by Jeff Tinsley, 84-18187/35.*

Page 86: A tearful vet is comforted during a visit to the Wall. *Photo by Sandra Rodger, 84-18130/15.*

Page 87: Falling on each others shoulders, vets share a special moment at the Memorial. *Photo by Dane A. Penland, 84-18155/33A.*

Pages 88–89: A lone veteran watches the dedication of the Memorial from the isolation of a nearby tree. The American flag is held by one of the thousands of spectators below. *Photo by Jeffrey Ploskonka, 82-13703/15.*

Page 89: While taps is played, vets at the Memorial honor the POWs and MIAs still unaccounted for. *Photo by John Steiner, 84-18099/29.*

Page 90: Bob Wieland, a vet who lost his legs in Vietnam, stands in his wheelchair to talk with fellow vets at the Memorial. *Photo by Jeffrey Ploskonka, 82-13705/15.*

Page 91: Three visitors to the Memorial share an emotional moment. *Photo by Jeffrey Ploskonka, 84-18201/23A.*

Page 92: Frequently seen at the Memorial, this shirt expresses a veteran's feelings about his Southeast Asian service. *Photo by Mark Avino, 84-18102/16A.*

Page 93: Three highly decorated veterans visiting the Memorial during the dedication ceremonies. *(Top) Photo by Dane A. Penland, 82-13692/22; (bottom left) Photo by Sandra Rodger, 84-18125/24; (bottom right) Photo by Mark Avino, 84-18105/8.*

Page 94: Vets pose for a group photo in front of the Memorial. *Photo by Jeffrey Ploskonka, 82-13705/7.*

Page 95: The informal honor guard, started by the vets themselves, stands watch at the Memorial during the dedication ceremonies. *Photo by Dane A. Penland, 82-13683/36.*

Page 96: The Sioux Indian ceremony held at the Memorial to induct Chuck Woolf into the tribe. *Photo by Dane A. Penland, 84-18159/10.*

Page 97: Chuck Woolf *(left)* and Tommy Roubideaux. *Photos by Dane A. Penland, (left) 84-18160/8 and (right) 84-18159/21.*

Page 98: Two vets at a reunion pose for a photograph. *Photo by Jeff Tinsley, 82-13726/21.*

Page 100, top: Smiling vet at one of the reunions held in Washington hotels during the week of the 1982 dedication. *Photo by Jeffrey Ploskonka, 82-13705/27.*

Page 100, bottom: A chance meeting between veterans in a hotel. *Photo by Dane A. Penland, 82-13674/14.*

Page 101: A vet scans pages of names of other veterans who registered at one of the many reunions held in Washington. *Photo by Jeff Tinsley, 82-13726/10.*

Page 102: Some of the hundreds of individual reunions that occurred the week of the 1982 dedication. *Photos by Jeff Tinsley, (top left) 82-13723/31; (top right) 82-13725/35; (bottom left) 82-13723/7; and (bottom right) 82-13739/29.*

Page 103: Some of the hundreds of individual reunions that occurred the week of the 1982 dedication. *Photos by Jeff Tinsley, (top left) 82-13725/32; (top right) 82-13723/6; (bottom left) 82-13739/30; and (bottom right) 82-13736/27.*

Page 104, top: Two vets pose for a reunion photograph. *Photo by Jeff Tinsley, 82-13737/8.*

Page 104, bottom: A group of veterans in wheelchairs meet during one of the unit reunions. *Photo by Jeff Tinsley, 82-13724/8.*

Page 105: Looking at a unit photo, veterans gather during a reunion in a Washington hotel. *Photo by Jeff Tinsley, 82-13723/8.*

Page 106, top: With a "thumbs-up" sign, a group of vets poses for a photo at the Memorial. *Photo by Richard Hofmeister, 84-18112/5A.*

Page 106, bottom: Two vets remember old times as they rest in the grass near the Memorial. *Photo by Dane A. Penland, 82-13686/21.*

Page 107: Through all the reunions surrounding events at the Memorial, there was continuing concern for the MIAs and POWs still unaccounted for. *Photo by Jeff Tinsley, 84-18188/29.*

Page 108: A sign worn by a vet looking for a friend. *Photo by Jeff Tinsley, 84-18190/6.*

Page 109: Signs worn by vets looking for friends or honoring lost comrades. *(Top) Photo by Aimee Hill, 82-136701A/12; (bottom) Photo by Mark Avino, 84-18104/39.*

Page 110: Two vets rush together in a reunion at the Memorial. *Photo by Jeffrey Ploskonka, 84-18201/19A.*

Page 111: Two veterans meet at the Memorial years after their service in Southeast Asia. *Photo by Jeff Tinsley, 84-18173/32.*

Page 112: Enjoying their party, a group of vets remember "the good times." *Photo by Jeff Tinsley, 82-13723/32.*

Page 113: During a party, Wolfman Jack, perhaps the best-known disc jockey of the Vietnam era, salutes the vets and pours them a drink. *Photos by Jeff Tinsley, (top) 82-13736/37 and (bottom) 82-13736/36.*

Page 114: Flickering candles stand out in the night during the 1984 candlelight service at the Memorial. *Photo by Jeffrey Ploskonka, 84-18198/32.*

Page 115: A night visitor takes a moment to meditate at the Wall. *Photo by Jeff Tinsley, 84-18175/8.*

Page 116: The soldier statue reflected in candlelight. *Photo by Jeffrey Ploskonka, 84-18198/15.*

Page 117: Pushing toward the Wall, the crowd at the 1984 candlelight service honors POWs and MIAs still unaccounted for. *Photo by Jeff Tinsley, 84-18177/31.*

Page 118: A veteran stands transfixed facing the Wall as his burning candle covers his hand with wax. *Photo by Jeff Tinsley, 84-18183/30.*

Page 119: A double amputee stands at the Wall during the candlelight service. *Photo by Jeff Tinsley, 84-18183/33.*

Pages 120–21: Candles and American flags reflected on the black granite wall. *Photo by Jeffrey Ploskonka, 84-18199/4.*

Page 123: Veterans testify during a hearing on post-traumatic stress. *Photos by Jeff Tinsley, (top) 82-13733/30 and (bottom) 82-13733/22.*

Page 124: A veteran testifies during an Agent Orange hearing. *Photos by Kim Nielsen, (top) 82-13663/12A and (bottom) 82-13663/18A.*

Page 125: An Agent Orange hearing in progress. *Photo by Kim Nielsen, 82-13663/22A.*

Page 126: The Unknown Soldier from the Vietnam War lies in state under the rotunda of the U.S. Capitol. *Photo by Howard Barbe, 84-5627/31.*

Page 128: An honor guard stands by, and the Unknown Soldier arrives at Washington's Andrews Air Force Base. *(Top) Photo by Eric James, 84-5639/34A; (bottom) Photo by Richard Hofmeister, 84-5643/19.*

Page 129: The coffin bearing the remains of the Unknown Soldier from the Vietnam War is carried down the Capitol steps. *Photo by Richard Brosnahan, 84-5638/22.*

Page 130: In momentary recognition of the Vietnam Veterans Memorial, the honor guard accompanying the procession of the Unknown Soldier does a left-face toward the Memorial. Immediately turning back, they continued the march to Arlington National Cemetery. *Photo by Jim Wallace, 84-5631/14.*

Page 131, top: A sailor salutes as the remains of the Unknown Soldier pass by. *Photo by Michael Klavans, 84-5620/10.*

Page 131, bottom: The caisson carrying the Unknown Soldier nears Arlington National Cemetery. *Photo by Eric James, 84-5640/5.*

Page 132: An informal group of Vietnam Veterans follows the procession for the Unknown Soldier as it nears Arlington National Cemetery. *Photo by Eric Long, 84-5634/35.*

Page 133, top: During the graveside services for the Unknown Soldier, Vietnam Veterans and families salute in Arlington National Cemetery. *Photo by Jeff Tinsley, 84-5611/26.*

Page 133, bottom: Vietnam vets march behind the formal procession in honor of the Unknown Soldier. *Photo by Jim Wallace, 84-5629/6A.*

Page 134: The caisson carrying the Unknown Soldier passes through Arlington National Cemetery toward the final resting place. *Photo by Eric Long, 84-5634/33.*

Page 135: The procession bearing the Unknown Soldier approaches Arlington National Cemetery. *Photo by Eric Long, 84-5634/27.*

Page 136: The remains of the Unknown Soldier are carried into the amphitheater at Arlington National Cemetery. *Photo by Richard Hofmeister, 84-5641/10.*

Page 137: President Ronald Reagan salutes the Unknown Soldier as the casket is carried by an armed forces honor guard at Arlington National Cemetery. The Congressional Medal of Honor was awarded during these ceremonies. *Photo by Richard Hofmeister, 84-5641/28.*

Page 138, top: Acting as the next of kin for the Unknown, President Reagan accepts the flag from the casket. *Photo by Jeff Tinsley, 84-5614/48A.*

Pages 138–39: A panorama of the graveside services for the Unknown Soldier. *Photo by Jeff Tinsley, 84-5616/7/8A.*

Page 140: Military officers salute the Unknown at the final resting place. *Photo by Jeff Tinsley, 84-5615/8.*

Page 141: A Vietnam vet salutes the Unknown during a long, emotional moment at the grave. *Photo by Jeff Tinsley, 84-5615/25.*

Page 143: A program from a high school reunion, saved and left at the Wall in 1986, two years after the event. *Photo by Richard Hofmeister, 86-7014/29.*

Page 144: Veteran Bob Wieland, who lost his legs in Vietnam, completes a walk across America to raise money for the hungry. *(Top) Photo by Jeff Tinsley, 86-5436/69A; (bottom) Photo by Richard Hofmeister, 86-5443/31.*

Page 145: The Veteran's Vigil Society, a group of vets standing vigil for unaccounted MIAs at the Memorial. *Photos by Jeffrey Ploskonka, (top) 84-8178/27 and (bottom) 84-8178/29.*

Page 146: Additional names are added to the Memorial. *(Top) Photo by Jeffrey Ploskonka, 86-9907/29; and (bottom) Photo by Richard Hofmeister, 86-9906/25.*

Page 147: A family member holds a rubbing made from one of the names added to the Memorial and dedicated during Memorial Day ceremonies in 1986. *Photos by Jeffrey Ploskonka, (top) 86-6472/29 and (bottom) 86-6471/27.*

Page 148: The organization No Greater Love participates in ceremonies commemorating the Tenth Anniversary of the Fall of Saigon. *(Top) Photo by Rick Vargas, 86-6477/22; (bottom) Photo by Richard Hofmeister, 85-7975/8.*

Page 149: Detail showing how names of those killed and those missing in action are listed on the Wall. *Photos by Jeff Tinsley, (top) 86-4564/2 and (bottom) 86-4564/28.*

Page 150: "Merry Christmas 'Angel Daddy,'" a card left at the Memorial on Christmas Morning, 1982. *Photo by Jeffrey Ploskonka, 86-9903/5A.*

Page 151: Taps, played during a service at the Memorial. *Photo by Rick Vargas, 86-6477/11.*

Pages 152–53: A father and son in Arlington National Cemetery. *Photo by Kim Nielsen, 82-13664/20.*

Page 159: Photographers Jeff Tinsley, Richard Hofmeister, Jeffrey Ploskonka, and Dane A. Penland. *Photo by Jim Wallace, 86-12516-3.*

The Photographers

The majority of the photographs in this book were taken by four photographers from the Smithsonian's Office of Printing and Photographic Services. Each spent countless days and nights recording these images on film, often becoming deeply involved both with the events and with the people.

To get the panoramic photographs of the Memorial's dedication and the burial of the Unknown Soldier, Jeff Tinsley carried a special camera in addition to his normal equipment. Waiting to photograph the Unknown Soldier (pages 138–39), he stood more than six hours in the rain.

Dane Penland traveled on his own to South Dakota to photograph the Sioux Sun Dance Ceremony with Chuck Woolf and Tommy Roubideaux, whom he had photographed after their emotional meeting at the Wall (page 97). When he was unable to take pictures because of tribal tradition, he participated in parts of the ceremony himself.

Jeffrey Ploskonka, whose double exposure taken in-camera at the dedication (page 5) has become a well-known poster, kept returning to the Memorial, often on his own. On one such visit early Christmas morning, he photographed "Merry Christmas 'Angel Daddy'" (page 150).

All were deeply moved by what they photographed. Their sentiments are perhaps best expressed by their supervisor, Richard Hofmeister, who photographed the grieving mother locating her son's name on the Wall (pages 54–57). "Deep inside," he said, "we all cried."

There are many other photographers from the Smithsonian's Office of Printing and Photographic Services whose work also appears here.

They include: Mark Avino, Howard Barbe, Richard Brosnahan, Michael Klavans, Eric Long, Kim Nielsen, John Steiner, Rick Vargas, and Jim Wallace.

Interns and volunteers whose photographs appear in this book include: Tracey Eller, Aimee Hill, Eric James, and Sandra Rodger.

Tinsley   Hofmeister   Ploskonka   Penland

Richard Hofmeister is Chief of the Special Assignment/Photography Branch. He has been a photographer with the Smithsonian since 1965. A native of Germany, he served in the U.S. Army during the Korean War.

Dane Penland has been a photographer with the Smithsonian since 1977. He was born at Patuxent Naval Air Test Station, Maryland.

Jeffrey Ploskonka has been a photographer at the Smithsonian since 1979. He was born in Detroit, Michigan, and is a graduate of Brooks Institute of Photography in Santa Barbara, California.

Jeff Tinsley has been a photographer at the Smithsonian since 1977. He was born in Washington, D.C., and served briefly with the U.S. Navy.

Acknowledgments

Producing this book and the photographs it contains would not have been possible without the help of many people.

From the beginning, the staff of the Vietnam Veterans Memorial Fund (VVMF) were of valued assistance providing access and information. In particular we want to thank Sandie Fauriol, who directed the 1982 National Salute to Vietnam Veterans and is now Executive Director of the Project on the Vietnam Generation. Throughout this undertaking, her counsel and guidance have been critical to our success. We also received invaluable help in 1982 from Karen (Bigelow) Doubek of the VVMF. A former staff member of the Smithsonian's Office of Printing and Photographic Services, she gave advice on events and their locations that led to many of the photographs presented here.

Also from the beginning, we have been indebted to Smithsonian Assistant Secretary for Administration John Jameson, who provided the underlying support and encouragement for the continued development of photographic historical documentation projects such as this.

Many of these photographs could not have been made without the cooperation of members of the U.S. Park Police, whose jurisdiction includes the Memorial. Their photographer, Charlie Pereira, has always been a friend and ally. Special thanks must go to Park Police Helicopter Pilot, Dwayne K. Darnell and Paramedic David R. Duffy. Both are Vietnam Veterans whose outstanding skills facilitated our aerial coverage.

In many cases, we needed to borrow camera equipment for special assignments during this project. It was always made available by Bill Pekela of Nikon Professional Services in New York, and Greg Smith of their Washington office, whose assistance is gratefully appreciated.

We thank Michael Winney of the U.S. Army Military History Institute in Carlisle Barracks, Pa., for his assistance in the development of this book; and Helen Wadsworth for her advice on picture selection.

From the Division of Armed Forces History, we thank Stephen L. Stewart for his work coordinating the text.

From the Office of Printing and Photographic Services, virtually everyone on the staff played an important role in the development and production of these photographs. We especially thank Lorie H. Aceto and Melissa Johnson for their invaluable assistance producing the hundreds of original prints from which the final selections were edited. In addition to the photographers whose credits appear with their work, printing of the final selections was provided by Louie Thomas of the Laboratory Staff; and Gail Mineo, a talented summer high school intern. Laurie Minor, a summer intern from James Madison University, also provided much of the laboratory printing and coordination. Without her assistance, production of the photographs would have been considerably more difficult.

From Stackpole Books, we thank Peggy Senko, Chet Fish, David Detweiler, and Richard King, whose skillful editorial advice and guidance can be seen throughout the philosophical development and presentation of this book.

Finally, we thank those who conceived of and built the Vietnam Veterans Memorial, and the Vietnam Veterans themselves, whose presence made it come alive. In so doing, they honored not only their fallen comrades but also themselves.

B-2

975.3   Reflections on the
R332   wall

              86023151

OCT 2 3 1987

RODMAN PUBLIC LIBRARY
215 East Broadway
Alliance, OH   44601